by Jennifer Poux

Grosset & Dunlap

GROSSET & DUNLAP
An Imprint of Penguin Random House LLC, New York

If you purchased this book without a cover, you should be aware that this book is stolen property. It was reported as "unsold and destroyed" to the publisher, and neither the author nor the publisher has received any payment for this "stripped book."

Penguin supports copyright. Copyright fuels creativity, encourages diverse voices, promotes free speech, and creates a vibrant culture. Thank you for buying an authorized edition of this book and for complying with copyright laws by not reproducing, scanning, or distributing any part of it in any form without permission. You are supporting writers and allowing Penguin to continue to publish books for every reader.

The publisher does not have any control over and does not assume any responsibility for author or third-party websites or their content.

Illustrations by Becky James

Photo credits: cover: (Serena Williams, Naomi Osaka) Julian Finney/Staff/Getty Images Sport/Getty Images North America, (Megan Rapinoe, Alex Morgan) Elsa/Staff/Getty Images Sport/Getty Images Europe, (Coco Gauff) DOMINICK REUTER/AFP/Getty Images

Copyright © 2020 by Penguin Random House LLC. All rights reserved. Published by Grosset & Dunlap, an imprint of Penguin Random House LLC, New York. GROSSET & DUNLAP is a registered trademark of Penguin Random House LLC. Printed in the USA.

Visit us online at www.penguinrandomhouse.com.

ISBN 9780593222539　　　　　　　　　　10 9 8 7 6 5 4 3 2 1

TABLE OF CONTENTS

•••••••••••••••••••••

PART I: WOMEN WHO HOLD COURT

> **CHAPTER 1:** The Legend: Serena Williams • 7
>
> **CHAPTER 2:** The Kid: Coco Gauff • 18
> Scoop! Extra: The History of Tennis Scoring
>
> **CHAPTER 3:** The Class Act: Naomi Osaka • 28
> Scoop! Quiz: Test Your Tennis Chops

PART II: A FIELD OF WOMEN

> **CHAPTER 4:** The Entertainer and Activist: Megan Rapinoe • 41
> Scoop! Extra: Brandi Chastain
>
> **CHAPTER 5:** The Star: Alex Morgan • 55

PART III: THE WOMAN WHO FLIES

> **CHAPTER 6:** Simone Biles: The Woman Who Flies • 67
> Scoop! Extra: Mary Lou Retton

PART IV: GOLDEN WOMEN

> **CHAPTER 7:** The Women Who Made Olympic History • 81
>
> **CHAPTER 8:** The Tokyo Games 2020 • 85
> Scoop! Quiz: The Ultimate Women in Sports

> **ANSWER KEY • 95**

PART I

WOMEN WHO HOLD COURT

CHAPTER 1

THE LEGEND: SERENA WILLIAMS

THE SCOOP! DEETS

BORN: September 26, 1981
SIGN: Libra
BIRTHPLACE: Saginaw, Michigan
MIDDLE NAME: Jameka
PARENTS: Oracene Price and Richard Williams
HUSBAND: Alexis Ohanian
DAUGHTER: Alexis Olympia Ohanian Jr. (called Olympia)
HEIGHT: 5'9"
COACHES: Parents and Patrick Mouratoglou
DIET: Vegan

A Rising Star

There can only be one queen in any sport. In tennis, that seat indisputably belongs to Serena Williams. You can argue that she might soon be dethroned by one of the young phenoms nipping at her Nike heels. (More on them later!) But even in the throes of a Grand Slam loss, Serena still reigns supreme as the best and most famous female tennis player in the world—and the richest. She is the ultimate competitor. And she's the most glam superstar of her sport, of any sport really. Serena Williams is a role model for women who value strength, excellence, and success. (And look good doing it.) And on top of all that, now she's a role model for working moms.

What makes Serena's story unique is that, unlike most of the tennis stars who preceded her, she comes from humble beginnings. Tennis was a country club sport for the white, privileged set until the Williams family smashed that tradition. Serena and her older sister, Venus, weren't born with golden rackets in their hands. They started training on public tennis courts in Compton, California. Yup. The Compton of movie and music fame.

"We literally took the globe and shook it, me

and Venus, because we came from Compton. We came from nothing. And in tennis you kind of have to be . . . you have to have something."

Serena and Venus were born in Saginaw, Michigan, to Richard Williams and Oracene Price. Richard has children from previous marriages and Oracene has three additional daughters. When Venus and Serena were little girls, their dad saw a tennis match on television and was blown away by the size of the winner's check, so he decided to teach himself the game. And then he decided to teach his daughters.

> **Here's the SCOOP!** Mr. Williams wrote a 78-page plan to teach his daughters tennis. Serious props to Dad!

When Serena was nine, the Williams family moved to West Palm Beach, Florida, where the girls could train at Rick Macci's tennis academy. But Serena and Venus didn't spend much time on the junior circuit like the other players. Their father believed they should spend more time on schoolwork. And they had witnessed some racism: He heard white parents saying nasty things about his daughters.

Turns out they didn't need to spend a lot of time on the junior circuit. When Venus was fourteen, she won her first professional match. And just three years later, she made the finals of her first US Open. With Venus suddenly getting national attention, Richard Williams told people Serena was the better player.

He was right.

Serena would eventually overshadow her big sis. When she was sixteen, she started playing professional tournaments. And by the time she was eighteen, she won the first Williams' family Grand Slam title at the US Open.

Did it get weird between them once Serena became the better player and bigger star? Maybe. They've both admitted it's awkward when they play each other. Someone has to win, and more times than not, it's advantage Serena. But they've played and won many doubles tournaments together as teammates. And Venus is always supportive of Serena, saying her first responsibility is as big sister. Serena has said, "Family's first and that's what matters most. We realize that our love goes deeper than the game."

Family goals!

But that doesn't mean Serena doesn't love the game. Puh-lease! The woman is passionate about tennis, and she has twenty-three Grand Slam wins in her crown to prove it! That's the most by any man or woman, post 1960s. She also holds the most singles, doubles, and mixed doubles tournament wins combined of any other tennis player playing today.

Scoop! Amazing Women in Sports

⬇ SOME SCOOP! CAREER HIGHLIGHTS ⬇

2000 — First Olympic gold medal.

2002 — First Wimbledon championship, ending the year with her first number one ranking.

2002–2003 — First "Serena Slam," winning the US Open, the Australian Open, the French Open, and Wimbledon consecutively. (These four make up the Grand Slam.)

2008 — Second Olympic gold medal.

2012 — Third and fourth Olympic gold medals.

2014–2015 — Second career "Serena Slam" at age thirty-three. (That's old for tennis.)

2017 — Defeats Venus at the Australian Open, winning twenty-third Grand Slam title. While she's two months pregnant!

★ The New Family ★

Serena Williams married Alexis Ohanian, one of the cofounders of Reddit, in New Orleans on November 16, 2017. Their wedding was the stuff of fantasies and fairy tales, fit for a queen. The theme: a French ball, in the style of *Beauty and the Beast*. (There was even a carousel brought in for the day!) And the queen herself wore a fantastic strapless princess ball gown and cape made by the couture house Alexander—wait for it—McQueen.

The most important guest? No, not Beyoncé—who was there. It was a tiny guest, wearing a white bejeweled dress. She was just over two months old.

On September 1, 2017, Serena gave birth to Alexis Olympia Ohanian Jr., named for her dad. Her parents call her Olympia. She looks like Mom, and of course she's totally adorbs. The baby, now toddler, already has nearly six hundred thousand Instagram followers!

> **Here's the SCOOP! At three months old, Olympia was the youngest person to make the cover of *Vogue* magazine.**

The story of how Serena and Alexis got together

is pretty romantic. The two were staying at the same fancy hotel in Rome—Serena for a tennis match, Alexis for business. One morning, he sat at a table next to hers in the dining room.

"I was so annoyed that he'd sat down next to me," she says. Awkward.

But then they started talking and a spark was lit.

> **Here's the SCOOP! with sprinkles: When they met, Alexis had never watched any of Serena's matches. And Serena had never heard of Alexis's company, Reddit.**

Serena invited Alexis to come to Paris to watch her play in the Paris Open, and he actually went! Eighteen months later, he flew her to Rome—to the same hotel and table where they'd met—to propose! (Love that!)

Now the glam fam spends their time together in Palm Beach, Los Angeles, New York, or globetrotting. And sometimes you can spot Dad and Olympia in the grandstands (with her famous doll Qai Qai, who has her own Insta) watching Mom play. That's one lucky kid!

 The Activist and Businesswoman

"The day I stop fighting for equality and for people that look like you and me will be the day I'm in my grave."

That was Serena's answer to a reporter's question during a press conference after she lost the 2019 Wimbledon final. She was asked about comments made by tennis great Billie Jean King that Serena should put her activism aside and focus on tennis.

Serena has written and spoken about the gender pay gap and how it affects women of color the most. She has been a UNICEF Goodwill Ambassador and has partnered with organizations to promote gender and racial equality. Serena uses her celebrity status to stand up for those who don't have her platform. Kudos for that!

Perhaps it's her very presence on the court and on the world stage that has the greatest effect on racial inequality. By any measure, Serena is a huge success story—and an incredible role model for girls and women of color.

But it hasn't always been easy for her. Serena has faced racism and other forms of verbal and written attacks as a professional tennis player.

In an interview with the rapper Common, Serena said she decided a long time ago not to read what people wrote about her. "I definitely was scrutinized because I was confident. I was black and I was confident. And I am black, I am confident."

And people would body-shame her (who would even dare?) because she was bigger and more muscular than other women, other athletes. "I'm okay to look them in their eye and say, if you don't like it, I don't want you to like it. I'm not asking you to like it. I like it and I love me."

She told Common with a laugh that her body is finally in style!

The Legend: Serena Williams

Speaking of her body, Serena created a clothing line to dress all body types, sold exclusively on her website. Her company, Serena, sells super cute sportswear, dresses, and coats. And she has a line called Serena GREAT, which sells clothing in sizes 1X to 3X for curvier bodies.

> **SCOOP! FACT**
> Serena's net worth is estimated at—wait for it—$189 million!!! Whoa.

Serena also does a lot of charity work and serves on corporate boards. The burning question: Where does she find the time?

CHAPTER 2

THE KID: COCO GAUFF

THE SCOOP! DEETS

BORN: March 13, 2004
SIGN: Pisces
HOMETOWN: Delray Beach, Florida
REAL NAME: Cori Gauff
PARENTS: Candi and Corey Gauff
SIBLINGS: Codey and Cameron
HEIGHT: 5'10"
IDOLS: Beyoncé, Rhianna, Michelle Obama, and the Williams sisters
FAVORITE MUSICIAN: Jaden Smith

Growing Up

Coco Gauff definitely won the athletic-gene lottery. Her parents, Corey and Candi Gauff, were both college athletes. Dad played hoops for Georgia State; Mom was a hurdler and heptathlete for Florida State. You get the picture.

Standing tall at five foot ten, Coco is powerful and hyper focused for a teenager.

> **SCOOP! FACT**
> A heptathlon is a track-and-field competition with seven events: 100-meter hurdles, high jump, shot put, 200-meter dash, long jump, javelin throw, and 800-meter run.

Coco may have won the awesome-family lottery as well. When Coco was seven, her parents realized she might be special and quit their jobs to devote themselves to her tennis career. And wow, were they right. Coco's dad became her coach, while her mom homeschooled her. And Coco has two younger brothers to keep her company/annoy her.

> **Here's the SCOOP!** Like the Kardashians, whose names all start with *K*, everyone in the Gauff family has the initials *CDG*. Too cute!

Coco's parents say she wasn't just athletic, she

was already able to concentrate for long periods of time in a way most kids her age couldn't. And she had drive. From an early age, she said she wanted to be the best in the world—even better than Serena.

Born in Delray Beach, Florida, Coco, whose real name is Cori (like her dad but with an *i*), lived in Atlanta for a while and then moved back to Delray with her family. Florida is where it's at for tennis phenoms—it's truly the youth tennis capital of the world. Serena Williams and Naomi Osaka both live and practice there. Hey, it's got year-round good weather and a zillion tennis academies.

But Coco didn't go the academy route. To some degree, her parents have followed the road map the Williams family created. Coco's dad has said that the Williams family paved the way for black tennis players, making it easier for the family to make the decision to go for it. Although every year since she was ten she has spent some time training at the Mouratoglou Academy in southern France—run by Serena Williams's coach, Patrick Mouratoglou—Coco's primary coach remains her dad. And they've decided to keep it in the family. That's not always easy.

"When I turned, I would say, twelve or thirteen, we used to argue. He used to be annoying because he would bring tennis home, and he's always around me," Coco told the *South Florida Sun-Sentinel*. "So now we talked, and we understand each other more now."

Dad might be annoying sometimes (can you relate?), but the family formula works for Coco. She had an awesome run on the junior circuit, reaching the girls' final of the junior US Open at age thirteen. The next year, she won the girls' final of the French Open and then the Orange Bowl tournament. By the time she reached the senior level at fifteen, she'd already racked up some impressive wins, and the tennis world noticed.

 Making a Splash

There was a particular moment when the world really started cheering Coco on. In 2019, the teen found herself holding a wild card for her first Grand Slam tournament: Wimbledon. Bam! Expectations were high for the fifteen-year-old, but how far could a kid really go at one of the most prestigious tournaments in the world?

Right out of the gate, Coco was slated to play one of her all-time idols: Venus Williams! Can you imagine? Her mom says they talked about one stroke, one game, one match at a time. But still—that's intense. Talk about pressure!

Yeah, well, she didn't just play Venus, she beat her decisively in two matches, 6–4, 6–4! She was the youngest player to win a match at Wimbledon since 1991. She followed that win with two more, and finally lost in the fourth round to Simona Halep, who would win the tournament. And when she left Wimbledon, her WTA ranking had shot up from 342 to 146! Eventually she'd make it to 68.

In the summer of 2019 in New York, Coco played at the US Open, where she was very popular with the crowd. A lot of stans came to see the child prodigy play on center stage. And she did not disappoint: Coco made it to the third round, where she was up against the woman ranked number one in the world: Naomi Osaka.

> **SCOOP! FACT**
> Wimbledon, which takes place every year at the All England Club in Wimbledon, London, on grass courts, is the oldest tennis tournament in the world. It started in 1877—that's 127 years before Coco was born!

Coco lost to Naomi 6–3, 6–0. But at the end of the match, something special happened, something unusual in the tennis world. You know when athletes shake hands at the end of a battle? Well, they did. But then Naomi invited Coco to share her on-court post-match TV interview. At first Coco was like, no way. But Naomi told her that speaking from experience, it was better to cry with the support of the crowd than alone in the locker room. It was a moment that made headlines around the world for twenty-one-year-old Naomi's compassion, and the composure with which the young new star handled the situation.

Coco talked about that experience with Naomi afterward at a press conference. "For me, the definition of an athlete is someone who on the court, I guess, treats you like your worst enemy, but off the court can be your best friend, and I think that's what she did today."

Coco was bummed to lose, but ultimately, it was the icing on the cake of an amazing year in the seniors. Tennis.com put it this way: "In June, the Atlanta native and Florida resident was a promising junior; by Labor Day, she was the future of American tennis, and she had leapt to the top of the sports-marketing heap. Team 8, Roger Federer's agency, represented her. New Balance rolled out an ad campaign, 'Call Me Coco,' and designed a striking dress for her to wear at the US Open. *Teen Vogue* featured her on its cover. Michelle Obama hung out with her. Even Beyoncé's mother, Tina Knowles-Lawson, professed herself a Coco fan on Instagram."

"I was, like, screaming," Coco said when she heard that.

Speaking of Insta, Coco's account, with nearly 620,000 followers, says: "I'm just a kid who has some pretty big dreams."

Just a kid? Not so much. And she hates when people dismiss her or anyone in her generation because of their age. She's interested in using her public platform to bring attention to issues like climate change.

"Lately, younger people are leading movements and I guess the world has to get used to it because we're used to older people telling us what to do," she told a newspaper.

But Coco isn't all tennis and serious issues. Like most teens, she loves music and can be found in the locker room wearing headphones before a match, listening to her faves. Jaden Smith tops her list.

Movies? She likes Marvel and horror.

Coco has a hoodie addiction. At Wimbledon, she was buying too many (she's got her own money now), but her mom banned her from buying more for two months. Otherwise, she says she really doesn't shop much. She can't buy a car yet because she doesn't drive!

What's she like to hang out with? Her doubles tennis partner Caty McNally calls her laid-back and easy to get along with. Sounds like a girl you can chill with. Off the court, that is. Don't mess with Coco when she's got a racket in her hands!

HERE'S THE SCOOP!

ON THE HISTORY OF TENNIS SCORING

What's all that love about, you ask? Why does tennis scoring start at 15? None of it seems to make sense. The origin of the wacky 15–30–40 scoring system is possibly medieval French. Some people think it has to do with the face of a clock. Another theory proposes that tennis scoring is based on a French game called *jeu de paume*, a precursor to tennis in which a traditional court was ninety feet long with forty-five feet on each side. When the server scored, she moved fifteen feet. Check. If the server scored again, she would move fifteen more feet. Check. If she scored again, she would only move ten feet. Check. Check.

So why "love" instead of "zero"? There's a theory it comes from the French word for "egg," *l'oeuf*, because an egg looks like the number zero. Makes sense, sort of!

CHAPTER 3

THE CLASS ACT: NAOMI OSAKA

THE SCOOP! DEETS

BORN: October 16, 1997
SIGN: Libra
BIRTHPLACE: Osaka, Japan
PARENTS: Tamaki Osaka and Leonard Francois
SIBLING: Mari
HOMETOWN: Boca Raton, Florida
HEIGHT: 5'11"
BOYFRIEND: YBN Cordae

 A Bit of Background

If you knew just one thing about Naomi Osaka before reading SCOOP!, it's probably that she beat Serena Williams at the 2018 US Open to win her first Grand Slam tournament. (More on that later!) Another memorable moment of Naomi Osaka's young career is what happened when she beat Coco Gauff at the US Open the following year, as we covered in Chapter 2. Naomi didn't win that tournament, but her humanity toward Coco singled her out as a different kind of player.

Naomi Osaka has been ranked number one in women's tennis, and she's one of the best in the world, with a mega career in front of her. But there's something about her quirky personality that makes her a standout off the court. It's a unique combination of shyness—a hesitation to say too much in interviews—and pure honesty. She can be awkward. And sometimes she's straight-up funny.

After a win in Beijing in 2019, Osaka spoke about her dad/coach at a press conference: "He's annoyed me so much that it just makes me angry and I use the anger as a fuel to win." Osaka laughed, but you couldn't help but think it was probably true. And then she retweeted the clip with this disclaimer: "All jokes aside I love my dad so much and I'm grateful for everything I learn from him on and off the court. I feel extremely lucky to be his kid cause he just drops knowledge."

All three tennis players profiled so far in this book have a couple things in common. One, they're all women of color in a traditionally white profession. And two, their coach is their dad and the person who set out to make them great tennis players. It's a strategy that worked for Serena and Venus, and it's working for Coco and Naomi, too: They watched the Williams family and took a page from their book. And none of these dads is a tennis player! (Maybe that's the key to their success?)

Like Coco, Naomi's father started coaching her at a young age, following Richard Williams's playbook.

Naomi's dad is from Haiti and her mom is from Japan. Naomi was born in Japan, but the family moved to Valley Stream, New York, when she was three. They moved to Florida when she was nine, for, yes, the tennis opportunities. She trained at a handful of academies in Florida, but her dad is still her primary coach.

The Class Act: Naomi Osaka

> **Here's the SCOOP!** In 2019, Naomi gave up her American citizenship and is now solely a Japanese citizen. She did it so she could represent Japan at the 2020 Summer Olympics.

Naomi told Japanese broadcaster NHK: "It is a special feeling to aim for the Olympics as a representative of Japan." And she said, "I think playing with the pride of the country will make me feel more emotional." (She's pretty much a pop star in Japan.)

But she has faced some racism in Japan, where people who are half Japanese, called "haafu," sometimes have to contend with bullying.

Wherever she lives and whomever she plays for, Naomi's a star. And it all kicked into gear in 2018, when she skyrocketed to fame and fortune.

SCOOP! FACT
In 2018, she was the second-highest-paid female tennis player behind Serena.

The Grandstand

First, Naomi won the prestigious Indian Wells tournament, making her the youngest winner there in ten years. Later that year she reached the third round at Wimbledon and the French Open, but it wasn't until the US Open that summer that she was on fire again. And in the final, she faced one of her all-time idols: Serena Williams. (She even did a report on her in third grade.) It was the second time she would play Serena; the first was in Miami months earlier when Naomi crushed her in straight sets. Savage!

It was a dream come true to play Serena in a Grand Slam, but it didn't play out the way she expected. In the first set, Naomi outserved and outhit Serena, winning it 6–2. In the second set, the chair umpire called a code violation on Serena for coaching; tennis coaches aren't supposed to coach from the stands. Serena disagreed with the umpire, telling him that she never cheats. And then Serena got frustrated during an Osaka point and slammed her racket onto the court, destroying it.

The Class Act: Naomi Osaka

The umpire issued a second code violation and then awarded Naomi a point. (You still following?)

Serena and the umpire got into a heated exchange, and the crowd, which was there to see Serena win her record-tying twenty-fourth Grand Slam, started booing. Serena demanded an apology for the accusation of cheating and called the umpire a thief for taking a point from her. More arguing ensued, and a third code violation was issued, resulting in a game loss for Serena. In the end, Naomi outplayed Serena throughout and won the second set 6–4 and the match!

Naomi never lost her cool. When she won, in what should have been a moment of celebration, the crowd continued to boo. The stadium was amped up with rage at the umpire. To her credit, Serena hugged Naomi and asked the crowd to stop booing.

> **Here's the SCOOP!** Naomi is the first Japanese player to ever win a Grand Slam.

What did Naomi think about it all? A few months later, she told *Time* magazine: "In a perfect dream, things would be set exactly the way you would want them. But I think it's more interesting that in real life, things aren't exactly the way you planned. And there are certain situations that you don't expect, but they come to you, and I think those situations set up things for further ahead."

That experience set her up to treat Coco Gauff with empathy and kindness when she beat her at the US Open a year later. Why did she decide to include Coco in her on-court interview after the match?

"I just thought about what I wanted her to feel leaving the court. Like, I wanted her to have her head high, not, like, walk off the court sad. I wanted her to be aware that she's accomplished so much and she's still so young." All the feels, Naomi!

So, what do you do with all the prize money and cash from sponsors like Citizen watches when you've just started adulting at twenty-one? You buy a house! And not just any crib. Naomi bought the Los Angeles home of one of SCOOP!'s recent subjects: Nick Jonas!

It's a beautiful, ultra-mod pad in a neighborhood known as the Beverly Hills Post Office. The house has five bedrooms, four bathrooms, and a pool. It doesn't have a tennis court. Guess she'll have to add that later.

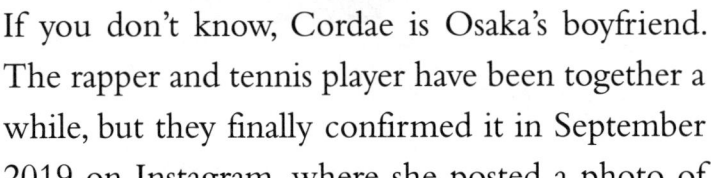

Here's the SCOOP! with sprinkles: Naomi paid a reported $6.91 million for it! Whoa.

Could the purchase have anything to do with the fact that YBN Cordae lives in LA? Just sayin'.

The Boyfriend

If you don't know, Cordae is Osaka's boyfriend. The rapper and tennis player have been together a while, but they finally confirmed it in September 2019 on Instagram, where she posted a photo of the two of them getting cozy beneath the famous Hollywood Sign. She wrote: "Very grateful you're in my life, always learning from you, always inspired by you. Also, always VERY entertained by you. Love ya kid."

On Naomi's birthday, Cordae posted on his account: "Happy Bday to my lil Supahstar @naomiosaka. You inspire me more ways than you know. Happy to have a real one."

Speaking of real, Naomi's been known to say things like, "I think everyone is cooler than me." Can't we all relate to that sometimes?

↓ TEST YOUR TENNIS CHOPS ↓

Take this quiz to test your tennis knowledge.

1. In what state is the annual Indian Wells tournament played? _____

2. Who defeated Bobby Riggs in the famous Battle of the Sexes? _____

3. In 1953, who became the first woman to win all four Grand Slam tournaments in the same year? _____

4. Name the four Grand Slam tournaments. (Bonus point for getting them in order!)

_____
_____
_____

5. What's the word for a serve that doesn't get returned? _____

6. Which young Canadian beat Serena Williams at the 2019 US Open?

_____

7. Who was the first African American woman to win Wimbledon?

_____

8. What are the primary surfaces on which professional tennis is played?

_____

9. Who was the first Russian to rank number one in the world by the Women's Tennis Association? _____

10. How many tennis balls are sold in the United States each year? _____

Check your answers on page 95.
How many did you get correct?

1-4 correct: Love

5-7 correct: 40

8-10 correct: Match

PART II
A FIELD OF WOMEN

CHAPTER 4

THE ENTERTAINER AND ACTIVIST: MEGAN RAPINOE

THE SCOOP! DEETS

BORN: July 5, 1985
SIGN: Cancer
MIDDLE NAME: Anna
TWIN: Rachael
HOMETOWN: Redding, California
COLLEGE: University of Portland
TEAMS: US Women's National Team and Seattle Reign FC
POSITION: Winger and midfielder
HEIGHT: 5'6"
GIRLFRIEND: Sue Bird

 In the Beginning

Sometimes being a professional athlete is more than just being the best on the field. It's often about what you do *off* the field, too. Here are two quotes that tell you a lot about Megan Rapinoe:

"I myself don't consider myself a soccer player. I consider myself an entertainer."

"Do what you can. Do what you have to do. Step outside yourself. Be more, be better, be bigger than you've ever been before."

Not a soccer player? Yeah, right. Megan Rapinoe is the world's best. But she's got a point: When she's out on the field, the woman knows how to entertain her fans. (Remember that iconic post-goal pose at the World Cup?) And when she's not on the field, but speaking in public, she knows how to grab your attention. As for the second quote, it's kind of the code by which she lives, a "go big or go home" mentality.

Megan hasn't always been the woke activist you see out there now talking about women's pay, LGBTQ rights, refugee rights, and other political issues.

In an interview with *Parade* magazine, she said, "I never grew up thinking about this stuff. I wasn't out in the streets marching as a kid."

Megan's the youngest of six kids, and she has a fraternal twin, Rachael, who used to be a professional soccer player, too. They grew up in Redding, California, in the northern part of the state.

> **SCOOP! FACT**
> Fraternal twins are not identical, but they can look a lot alike.

As a kid, Megan was really into—wait for it—soccer. She idolized her older brother who played, and she wanted to emulate him. So she started playing soccer at three! For most of her childhood until high school, her dad coached her teams. (Are we starting to see a trend here or what?!) In high school, she ran track and played basketball for some of her years at Foothill High School. But she played club soccer for the Elk Grove Pride.

> **Here's the SCOOP!** Megan was one of those kids who excelled in sports and school, and she and her twin were recruited with full scholarships to play soccer for the University of Portland Pilots.

The ~~Rock~~ Soccer Star

Soccer's important, but let's talk about Megan's look for a sec. Her vibe can be more rock star than soccer player off the field. Even on the field with her purple, pink, or white-blond hair, Megan looks like the lead singer of a band. And she pulls it off.

The Entertainer and Activist: Megan Rapinoe

> Here's the SCOOP! Did you know Megan and three other professional soccer players started a gender-neutral lifestyle brand in 2019? It's called Re-Inc.

Around the 2019 World Cup, her short purple do seemed to change color by the day. One game it was more violet, another more a pinkish hue.

And the outfits: a white men's-style suit with pink piping down the sleeves, a very revealing black-tie evening blazer with no shirt underneath, the John Lennon-esque sunglasses.

Is Megan channeling the actor Tilda Swinton or the rock god David Bowie? Whatever she's going for, she knows how to work it. You can always find her on the field—just look for her head!

And you can find her on the cover of *Glamour*. The magazine named her one of their Women of the Year in 2019—the "Champion" award! In her photo shoot, she's standing on a boat in the Hudson River, the Statue of Liberty behind her, wearing a white suit, no shirt, and yes, her hair is purple. Perfection.

So, soccer. Megan is a two-time FIFA World Champion (2015 and 2019) and an Olympic gold medalist (2012). She is cocaptain of the US Women's National Team and the Seattle Reign FC. Since graduating from the University of Portland, Megan has played professionally for the Chicago Red Stars, Philadelphia Independence, MagicJack, Sydney FC, Seattle Sounders Women, and Olympique Lyonnais.

It's the US Women's National Team and the Olympics that turned her into an international celeb. And the funny thing is, she really wasn't a megastar until the 2019 World Cup, when she was thirty-four. That's not so young in sports. Usually an athlete's star power doesn't reach maximum wattage when they're in their mid-thirties.

But it was her event: She finished the World Cup with six goals and three assists. Pinoe, as some of her teammates call her, was awarded the Golden

The Entertainer and Activist: Megan Rapinoe

Ball and the Golden Boot. And she struck a pose seen around the world—arms outstretched, closed-mouth smile—a pose that seemed to simply say, "Victory!"

The Girlfriend

Only a power couple can claim they met at a 2016 Olympic photo shoot in Rio de Janeiro! Megan says she was introduced to Sue Bird and made a stupid joke, then felt bad. (Relatable!) Then at an after-party for the USA Basketball Women's National Team, they talked and realized they both lived in Seattle. And when they got home, they started dating.

Sue Bird is a guard for the Seattle Storm of the WNBA. She's from Syosset, New York, and is a two-time NCAA champion who played for UConn.

She's five years older and a few inches taller than Megan. Who's the better athlete? That's a toss-up. Together they have five Olympic gold medals. But the women say neither is jealous of the other's career.

"We are huge fans of each other. I have become, like, a Seattle Storm number one superfan, of course," Megan told *People* magazine.

> **Here's the SCOOP! Sue says Megan is an excellent dancer!**

They obviously have a lot in common, but there are clear differences in their personalities. Sue says Megan is more outgoing. Sue's shy. Sue dips her toe in the water—Megan dives in.

It took Sue a little longer to be open about their relationship. Megan has been outspoken about her sexuality for years. Sue told ESPN she wasn't hiding anything—her friends and family knew she was gay—but she was quiet in the public sphere until Megan convinced her that not hiding is different than coming out.

"Being around Megan, I learned that. And then

after I came out, just seeing the reactions, having people come up to me directly. I think there's just something really powerful about that."

Megan and Sue were the first same-sex couple to appear on the cover of *ESPN the Magazine*'s Body Issue. #rolemodels

 The Advocate

Megan realized she was gay in college. "I think as soon as I figured it out I was like, this is awesome. My life has totally started. And I'm, like, ready to roll." Love the positivity!

She says if not for being gay, she'd just be another member of the white 1 percent, aka a wealthy, privileged white person. But being gay has helped her see issues of discrimination through another lens.

"I'm asking people to be allies for us [women's soccer] or be allies for me as a gay woman, and then in turn it's my responsibility to be an ally for other people as well, even if I don't have intimate experiences with the things that they are talking about," she told *Parade* magazine.

She took a knee during the national anthem at an international soccer match to support Colin Kaepernick, the former NFL player protesting the oppression of black people and other minorities, and has spoken about him publicly. And she took on the president of the United States, which turned into a short Twitter battle. She can be a lightning rod, and she owns it. And if the best revenge is living well, score one for Megan: The US Women's National Team won the World Cup shortly afterward.

Megan is also the cochair of When We All Vote, working with Michelle Obama to encourage people to register to vote. Check out their cool "voting squad" ads.

Her biggest cause at the moment is gender equality. Megan and twenty-eight members of the US Women's National Team filed suit in 2019 against the US Soccer Federation for gender

The Entertainer and Activist: Megan Rapinoe

discrimination and unequal pay. You'd think after the team won the 2019 World Cup it wouldn't be an issue. (The US men didn't even make it to the World Cup and they're paid more.) Even the crowd at the stadium in France chanted "Equal pay" after the American women won.

> Here's the SCOOP! The prize money for the 2019 Women's World Cup was $30 million and the champions got about $4 million. The prize money for the Men's World Cup was $400 million and the champions took home about $38 million.

The huge World Cup win and Megan's comments and speeches following it brought national attention to the issue and support from politicians and celebrities.

"We did this whole World Cup thing, won it. Did everything above and beyond. And, like, now we have to go in a room and try to convince people that we're worth it, as if it's not already crystal clear." Fire.

It *is* crystal clear. And hopefully justice will come down on their side. The team is certainly fighting the good fight.

But Megan's message really isn't about fighting. It's about being good to each other, as she told a cheering NYC crowd after the ticker-tape parade for the World Cup team in 2019. "We have to be better. We have to love more, hate less. We gotta listen more and talk less."

That's how Megan Rapinoe rolls.

BRANDI CHASTAIN

Before Megan Rapinoe and her victory pose, there was Brandi Chastain: an American soccer player who made a big splash at the 1999 World Cup championships. She nailed the fifth kick of the penalty shoot-out against China in the tournament's final match, giving the United States the championship win. In celebration, she whipped off her jersey and fell to her knees in her black sports bra. It became the iconic image of the World Cup that year, and one of the most famous photos ever taken of a female athlete. Men had been taking off their jerseys for years, but of course when Brandi did it, it got a lot more attention. The next year, FIFA changed the rules, making it a yellow-card offense for a man or woman to remove their jerseys in celebration.

Chastain said of the sports bra moment seen around the world that it was "momentary insanity, nothing more, nothing less. I wasn't thinking about anything. I thought, 'This is the greatest moment of my life on the soccer field.'"

CHAPTER 5

THE STAR: ALEX MORGAN

THE SCOOP! DEETS

BORN: July 2, 1989
SIGN: Cancer
MIDDLE NAME: Patricia
MARRIED NAME: Alexandra Morgan Carrasco
HOMETOWN: Diamond Bar, California
SIBLINGS: Jeri and Jeni
HUSBAND: Servando Carrasco
COLLEGE: UC Berkeley
TEAMS: Orlando Pride and US Women's National Team
POSITION: Forward
HEIGHT: 5'7"

 Girl on the Rise

Alex Morgan is that soccer player so many little girls look up to. Why? That's a no-brainer. She's one of the best players in the world

Scoop! Amazing Women in Sports

and one of the most famous. She's camera ready, with her long brown ponytail and radiant smile. And she comes off as an approachable person off the field, too!

Alex was once that little girl, looking up to players like Mia Hamm and Brandi Chastain. And she knew early on what she wanted to do with her life. Alex's mom saved a sticky note she wrote to her when she was just eight.

Hi Mommy! My name is Alex and I am going to be a proffesional athlete for soccer!

(Mind blown!)

Alex was a multisport athlete, and she played AYSO (American Youth Soccer Organization) soccer when she was a kid; her dad was often her coach. She says her dad was key to helping her reach her goals. (Where have you heard that before?!) In her memoir, *Breakaway: Beyond the Goal*, she wrote that her dad would tell her, "You're the best, but you can be better."

And she says he knew how much pressure to apply and when to back off. "He always kind of pushed me the right amount. And I feel like that's important for parents to see that it's okay to push kids into something but not too much. You want them to naturally gravitate toward something. So that's why I think me and my dad have such a great relationship."

She started playing club soccer late for a pro—she was fourteen when she joined Cypress Elite. And she played for her hometown school team, Diamond Bar High School, where she was named an All-American and was a three-time all-league pick. Alex also played for the Olympic Development Program.

In college, Alex played for the UC Berkeley team, the California Golden Bears. That was the move: She was a star there, leading the Bears to the NCAA tournament all four years. And she was tied for third on her school's list of all-time scorers, with forty-five goals. It's also where she met her future husband, soccer player Servando Carrasco. (More on him in a minute!)

The rest is history. A lot of it. Alex has played in three women's World Cup tournaments, and now she holds two championships. At twenty-two, she was the youngest player on the team in the 2011 World Cup. Her teammates called her Baby Horse. Now Megan Rapinoe says she's a "full-on stallion." The stallion is also an Olympic gold medalist as a member of the 2012 team.

In 2019, she once again earned the fandom of little girls—and bigger girls, boys, men, and women—at the World Cup as cocaptain with Megan Rapinoe and Carli Lloyd. The American women won, of course, and Alex was awarded the

Silver Boot for her six goals and three assists.

Now she plays for the Orlando Pride, and she hopes to play in the 2020 Olympics.

> **Here's the SCOOP!** Alex has had 107 career goals plus 43 assists, and still counting!

What would Alex say to all the young adults who adore her?

"No matter where you're at in life, or what you are trying to accomplish, people will always have their opinions. Listen to yourself, listen to your gut, and listen to the people in your life that you trust. Let your passion be your guide."

Sage advice.

 ## The New Family

As of this writing, Alex is due to give birth to a baby in the spring of 2020. You gotta love sports marriages. The gene pool is fire! I mean, can you imagine if the Carrasco kid doesn't like soccer or have a golden foot? Impossible.

Getting ahead of ourselves here—Alex Morgan married Servando Carrasco in Santa Barbara, California, on New Year's Eve, 2014. (So romantic!)

> **Here's the SCOOP!** The menu at their wedding reception included quesadillas and homemade churros, a nod to Servando's Mexican heritage.

The two met in college and now they both play soccer professionally. And they're both drop-dead gorgeous! Here's the kicker (pun intended): They play in different cities. Servando plays midfielder for the LA Galaxy, and Alex plays for the Orlando Pride and the US Women's National Team. It's not easy managing a long-distance marriage, but they do it. And they show up when it matters. Maybe you caught the kiss Servando gave his wife from the stands after her World Cup win in 2019.

Alex says she feels so lucky to be married to Servando. "We are both so happy, grateful, and excited to start our lives together as Mr. and Mrs. Carrasco," she told *People* magazine. "I truly married my best friend."

If you stalk Alex on Instagram, you've seen the cute husband-and-wife pics. You gotta love the beach wedding photo and her stunning dress. Wedding goals!

More recently on Insta, the happy couple announced to the world they're expecting a baby. They're standing on a rocky beach, Alex in a long pink sweater dress, Servando in a white T-shirt and jeans, his arm around his wife. He's holding a baby onesie that says: "Ready or not." And she's holding a sign that says: "Baby girl, April 2020." Too cute!

On Servando's Insta, he wrote: "Can't wait to meet my baby girl!" next to another pic from the couple's maternity shoot. This time, their dogs are in the frame wearing bandanas. One reads: "Baby human coming April 2020"; the other says: "I didn't sign up for this!" Those dogs are going to be jealous.

> **SCOOP! FACT**
> Alex and Servando have two dogs, Blue and Kiona, both rescue pups they adopted.

Maybe now that their family is growing, Alex and Servando will find a way to live full-time in the same city. In the meantime, they've kept their day jobs. In addition to soccer, Alex is a very busy woman.

All the Other Things She Does

Athletes must have ten times more energy than everyone else because it's astounding how much they manage to pack into their lives on top of their sport and their families. (Can you say overbooked?) Alex Morgan is no exception.

Alex advocates for a number of issues. Like her buddy Pinoe, she is participating in the soccer gender discrimination suit, and the two women are often interviewed together on the subject.

Outside of advocating for the women of soccer, Alex has favorite causes. "The main focus is kids and animals. I do a lot of work with Boys & Girls Clubs, and I'm an ambassador for UNICEF. I also support the ASPCA, because I am passionate about giving animals a voice. I even adopted a vegan diet, because it didn't feel fair to have a dog I adore, and yet eat meat all the time."

Alex says she is very conscious about what she eats. Eating a plant-based diet means you have to plan in advance—you can't just grab any sandwich or junk food when you're hungry. (Sounds like work!) She loves Mexican cuisine, and sometimes she'll live large and eat a burrito or tacos. Or a slice of pizza. (Hold the cheese.) But not on game days.

It's her job to be fit on the field and that helps in magazine shoots. Somehow Alex managed to squeeze in a *Sports Illustrated* Swimsuit Issue shoot in St. Lucia in 2019. (It's her second one.) Nice gig!

Why does she do it?

"I feel, like, empowered," she said in a *Sports Illustrated* interview. "Because I feel like I'm alongside so many incredible women and I think, like, being a part of *Sports Illustrated* Swim shows how incredible all these women can be in the confidence that you have to express yourself and be, like, vulnerable yet confident in who you are."

She should feel good. *Sports Illustrated* put her on the cover!

After their World Cup victory, Alex and Megan were featured on the cover of a regular *Sports Illustrated* issue. Alex has also graced the covers of *Time*, *Health*, and *Self* magazines.

Speaking of covers, she has a bunch of her own. Alex is a published author! You may have seen her book series, The Kicks. It's a middle-grade series about, what else? Girls who play soccer.

And of course Alex has had a number of

sponsorship deals with companies like Nike, Chobani, Panasonic, ChapStick, AT&T, Coca-Cola, and McDonald's. (The last two seem a little surprising for a healthy vegan!)

Alex is somewhat of a fashionista. Her Instagram is filled with shots of her wearing gorgeous evening gowns. That's what happens when you're one of the world's most famous athletes—you gotta show up to take home all those awards!

PART III

THE WOMAN WHO FLIES

CHAPTER 6

SIMONE BILES: THE WOMAN WHO FLIES

THE SCOOP! DEETS

BORN: March 14, 1997
SIGN: Pisces
MIDDLE NAME: Arianne
BIRTHPLACE: Columbus, Ohio
CITIZENSHIP: US and Belize
SIBLINGS: Adria, Ashley, Tevin
CURRENT RESIDENCE: Spring, Texas
HEIGHT: 4'8"
FAVORITE EVENT: Floor
SIGNATURE MOVES: The Biles I and Biles II
BOYFRIEND: Stacey Ervin Jr.
FAVORITE VACATION SPOT: Belize

In the Beginning

Simone Biles makes everything she does look easy. Triple-double on floor? No problem. Double-double dismount off the beam? No sweat.

Of course, none of it is remotely easy. Sure, she was born with mad talent. But Simone has logged long, grueling days for years to get that jaw-dropping air and land her death-defying dismounts.

The truth is, Simone didn't have an easy start in life. Her birth mother suffered from drug addiction, and when she was just three, Simone was taken away from her mother and placed in foster care along with her siblings. For about three years, she "bounced around" from one home to another.

"Although I was young when my foster care ordeal began, I remember how it felt to be passed off and overlooked," Simone wrote in an opinion piece for CNN. "Like nobody knew me or wanted to know me. Like my talents didn't count, and my voice didn't matter."

It must have been brutal. But then Simone got lucky: When she was six, her grandparents, Ron and Nellie Biles, adopted her and her sister Adria. (Her other sister, Ashley, and brother, Tevin, were adopted by their aunt in Ohio.) They created a warm, loving home for their new family in Spring, Texas. And when they realized Simone had a true gift, they went all in. You gotta love Ron and Nellie.

> **Here's the SCOOP!** Simone Biles's story really springs into action the day her school took a field trip to Bannon's Gymnastix in Houston, Texas, when she was six.

You ever dream that someone will catch you walking down the street or hear you sing and turn you into a model, actor, or music star? (Come on, admit it!) That's low-key what happened to Simone.

"I imitated the other gymnasts, and Coach Ronnie noticed. The gym sent home a letter requesting that I join tumbling or gymnastics."

That school trip was seriously serendipitous, and it marked the beginning of a legendary career.

The GOAT Highlights

Simone Biles truly is the greatest gymnast of all time. (That's not up for debate!) She sealed that title at the World Artistic Gymnastics Championships in 2019. There are so many firsts leading up to that competition, it would take an entire book to write about all of them.

But let's rewind to 2013, before Simone is a household name. She's just sixteen and already a powerhouse.

> **Here's the SCOOP!** She said in an interview years later that she didn't realize how talented she was until she started competing at the senior level. It sure was obvi to everyone else!

Watching her vault at the world championships that year, you can see the precision, the air, the speed. She wins silver on that event. On floor, where she wins gold, she's the charmer, the performer, big

Simone Biles: The Woman Who Flies

smiles. And her tumbling passes are incredible. On beam, the smile is gone—she is all business. She escapes a near fall and does not look happy when the routine is over. But she still wins bronze. She is crowned all-around champion that year.

In 2014, Simone becomes the first woman since 1974 to win four medals at a world championship! Simone keeps racking up the wins in 2015 as the world all-around champ (of course) and the US all-around champ, with gold, silver, and bronze medals in all events except uneven parallel bars. (She can't be perfect at everything!)

By the time 2016 rolls around, Simone is one of the premier names in world gymnastics. And it's no surprise when she makes the US women's Olympic team. Expectations are high and the pressure is on at the Summer Games in Rio de Janeiro, Brazil. The world is watching, and yes, Simone delivers, big-time! She is the vault and floor gold medalist, takes bronze on beam, and is the all-around winner. The icing on the cake? The

Final Five take home the team gold. Simone leaves Rio a huge star.

How do you top that? Well, first you take a year off, travel, become a contestant on *Dancing with the Stars*, hang out with your new bae (more on him later!), and then return better than ever.

"Coming back, I'm doing this just for me, and I think that's different than the last time around. For me I feel like I have nothing to prove to anyone, so I think that's what keeps me in this sport besides love and passion."

Simone hit the ground running after her hiatus. In 2018, she was crowned world all-around champion. And in 2019, she won the world championships yet again and was champion on floor, beam, and vault! By the end of the October competition in Stuttgart, Germany, Biles had collected a lifetime twenty-five world medals, the most in gymnastics history—nineteen of them gold, another world record! Oh, and just because she's that awesome, Simone now has two signature moves named for her: the Biles I and Biles II. That's the GOAT for you!

 The Boyfriend

Teenage Simone had a famous crush on Zac Efron—a life-size cardboard cutout of the actor hung out in her room, once upon a time. And remember when NBC surprised the Final Five at the 2016 Olympics with Zac in the flesh? Zac's old news now.

Can you think of a better match for the GOAT than another gymnast—a totally hot gymnast? Who else could keep up with her? Simone's boyfriend is Stacey Ervin Jr., former NCAA champion gymnast and WWE wrestler. Now he's an online health and fitness coach and podcaster. And on his Twitter account, he calls himself an acrobat.

Born in 1993, Stacey is four years older than Simone. He's Gen Y to Simone's Gen Z. The two met at the P&G Gymnastics Tournament about three years before they started dating in 2017. When Simone's mom hired Stacey to be a coach at World Champions Centre, their family-owned gym in Spring, Texas, the two got cozier.

> **Here's the SCOOP! First date: sushi. It's not Simone's thing, but Stacey pushed her out of her comfort zone and she was cool with it.**

On his birthday in September 2019, Simone posted a photo on Insta of the couple surrounded by sunflowers with this caption: "Happy birthday to the man of my dreams ♥. So many things I love about you. Your energy lights up an entire room. You're a true gentleman and you always put others first! Your mindset, grit and your passion for greatness. 26 will be a great one! Never stop being you Stacey Ervin Jr. I love you. 224."

All the feels!

On his Instagram, Stacey posted a shot of the adorable couple holding each other, their foreheads touching, eyes closed. He wrote: "Our hearts speak the same language. I'll always love you." And after her world championship wins in Stuttgart, he posted in all caps: "MY WOMAN IS A 5X WORLD CHAMPION IN THE ALL-AROUND & I COULDN'T BE MORE PROUD!"

Relationship goals!

Wedding bells, anyone?

Tough Times

Simone Biles has a pretty sweet life these days. But world champions experience personal pain just like the rest of us, and Simone has had more than her share.

You may have heard of Larry Nassar, the former doctor for the USA Gymnastics women's team who is spending the rest of his life in prison for sexually assaulting hundreds of girls in his care.

Simone, her 2016 Olympic teammate Aly Raisman, and many other gymnasts bravely came forward to accuse Larry Nasser of abuse, which ultimately led to his conviction. At first, as some of her friends began speaking out against their former physician, Simone did not reveal that she was a victim of Nassar. She went public for the first time on Twitter:

"I am not afraid to tell my story anymore. I too am one of the many survivors that was sexually abused by Larry Nassar. Please believe me when I say it was a lot harder to first speak those words out loud than it is now to put them on paper. There are many reasons that I have been reluctant to share my story, but I know now it is not my fault."

Once she found her voice, Simone became a powerful spokesperson for survivors of sexual assault, especially her fellow gymnasts. In an emotional interview ahead of the 2019 US Gymnastics Championships, she was asked about a Congressional investigation finding that the US Olympic Committee and USA Gymnastics knowingly hid Larry Nasser's abuse.

"It's hard coming here for an organization, having had them fail us so many times, and we had one goal and we've done everything they asked us for, even when we didn't want to. And they couldn't do one damn job. You had one job. You literally had one job and you didn't protect us."

More proof that Simone is not only physically strong, but mentally tough, too.

She would need to draw on her strength again shortly after the Kansas championships, when her older brother, Tevin Biles-Thomas, was arrested and charged with killing three people at a party in Ohio.

Simone tweeted: "My heart aches for everyone involved, especially for the victims and their families. There is nothing that I can say that can heal anyone's pain, but I do want to express my sincere condolences to everyone affected by this terrible tragedy. I ask everyone to please respect my family's privacy as we deal with our pain."

That is a lot of pain for anyone to deal with.

But in the true spirit of the champion she is, Simone showed up at the World Championships in Stuttgart, Germany, less than two months later and rocked it. And now she's got her sights on Tokyo 2020!

MARY LOU RETTON

It's never the athletic ability alone that makes a sports celebrity. Americans like to fall in love with an athlete—someone with personality, charm, and let's face it, the look. In the early 1980s, Mary Lou Retton was that girl. In fact, she was nicknamed "America's Sweetheart."

At the Los Angeles Olympics in 1984, Mary Lou became the first American gymnast to win gold in the all-around competition. She also took home two silvers and two bronze medals. But Mary Lou had something else: golden charm. Her smile was huge, and she lit up in front of the cameras. She was adorable and tiny at four foot nine, but her personality was oversized, and Americans fell hard for her.

PART IV
GOLDEN WOMEN

CHAPTER 7

THE WOMEN WHO MADE OLYMPIC HISTORY

There is a rich history in the United States of powerhouse women athletes who break speed records and gender stereotypes at the Olympics. That "greatest of all time" label is a tricky one—it usually means the person who received the most medals. But there are also the women who rammed through individual and cultural barriers who deserve praise. Here's a look at some of the Americans who did both.

 Wilma Rudolph, aka the Black Gazelle

How often do you hear about athletes overcoming paralysis to become Olympians? Exactly. Wilma, who was one of twenty-two siblings, had polio and scarlet fever as a kid in Tennessee and couldn't even walk for a good chunk of her childhood. But by the time she was sixteen, she was competing in track-and-field events in the Olympics! Four years later, Wilma was the first woman to win three gold medals in the Rome Olympics. She became an international star and a role model, especially for black athletes.

 Florence Griffith Joyner, aka Flo-Jo

She wasn't just fast, she shattered records in the 100-meter and 200-meter sprints in 1988. And her records still stand to this day! Flo-Jo is considered the fastest woman of all time. She was also known for her style, wearing running suits with one leg and bright colors and patterns. As for her fingernails, at the 1988 Olympics they were six inches long and painted red, white, blue, and gold. They matched her medals! Sadly, Flo-Jo died too young, at thirty-eight, of an epileptic seizure in her sleep.

Bonnie Blair

If you've never watched speed skating, you gotta check it out. Both long-track and short-track. They are thrilling events. And Bonnie Blair, a women's speed skater, did both. She grabbed America's attention on the ice and off with her big smile and girl-next-door vibe. And she grabbed tons of medals: She is one of the most decorated Olympic athletes in history with five gold medals and one bronze.

Gertrude Ederle

You've probably never heard of Gertrude. But she was a pioneer in the truest sense. First, she won three gold medals in swimming at the Paris Olympics in 1924. That would have been enough to grant her greatness status. But then two years later, she became the first woman to swim across the English Channel! And she did it two hours faster than any of the five men who completed the swim before her. Awesome! To top it off, Gertrude swam the Channel in a two-piece swimsuit. That was a gutsy first!

 Lindsey Vonn

She doesn't hold the Olympic medal record in downhill skiing—that goes to Andrea Mead Lawrence and Mikaela Shiffrin; Mikaela still competes. But Lindsey was the first American woman to win Olympic gold in the sport. And she has more Alpine Ski World Cup victories—eighty-two!—than any other female skier. It hasn't been easy: Lindsey has suffered a number of spectacular, televised crashes on the slopes. But she always races back. In 2019, at the age of thirty-four, she decided to hang it up. But she will not be forgotten in this daredevil sport.

CHAPTER 8

THE TOKYO GAMES 2020

*V*ictory and defeat are the two most certain results you'll see at the Olympics. Some of those victors will be surprises—they'll become America's newest darlings. And some of those defeats will come from the competitors the country banked on. It's inevitable. Here's a short list of a few women expected to continue their tremendous trajectories in the world of Olympic sports, and a few new ones who could take the Olympic Games by storm.

 Caroline Marks

Not only would Caroline be new to the Olympics, her sport will be new to the Games in 2020:

surfing. Get stoked! The competition for just two spots for US women will be tough—but eighteen-year-old Caroline has been an epic competitor since she was the youngest surfer to qualify for the championship tour in 2017 at just fifteen years old. Totally rad! Caroline grew up in Florida with a surf break across the street from her house. Dude! She's homeschooled to make room for competitions, and in her spare time she's into motocross.

 Katie Ledecky

Nothing new here—this swimmer is already an Olympic veteran, and she is savage! Katie has won five Olympic gold medals and fifteen world championship golds, the most ever for a female swimmer. And she holds the world records in the 400-, 800-, and 1500-meter freestyles. Barring disaster, Katie will be at the 2020 Games, and she could dominate again. Maybe she'll even break her own records! Katie grew up in Maryland and swam for Stanford University. She says she has always set clear goals for herself, then finds a way to realize them.

 Sunisa Lee, Kara Eaker, Jade Carey, Grace McCallum, MyKayla Skinner

Only three of these women will join Simone Biles on the 2020 US Olympic women's gymnastics team. Sunisa Lee is the young sensation who catapulted out of the junior division into second place behind Simone at the 2019 nationals and US selection competition. She is the national champion on uneven bars and one to watch closely. Kara Eaker is a serious medal contender on the beam. Jade Carey is the 2017 world silver medalist on floor and vault. Under new rules, the team can only have five members, but gymnasts can compete individually, and Carey is hoping to do that in 2020. Grace McCallum was third in the all-around at the 2019 nationals. Her event is floor. MyKayla Skinner is an NCAA gymnast at the University of Utah who specializes in floor and vault. Morgan Hurd was considered a frontrunner for the US team and the 2020 Games, but at the selection camp in the fall of 2019, she was only chosen as an alternate. Stay tuned.

 Allyson Felix

The champion track-and-field sprinter is on track (pun intended) to compete in the 2020 Olympic Games. She's a veteran of five Olympics! And she says this will be her last. The new mom had a very difficult pregnancy, and her baby girl, born in 2019, came two months early, which meant she spent a long time in the hospital. Allyson says the experience tested her strength. But she is getting back up to speed for Tokyo. She competes in the 100, 200, and 400 meters and 4×100 relay, and she has already amassed six Olympic gold medals and three silvers!

The Tokyo Games 2020

 Brighton Zeuner

Aside from having the coolest name around, Brighton is an Olympic contender in another new sport for 2020: skateboarding. The California girl would be one of the youngest competitors at the Olympics, having just turned sixteen. In 2017, she won the gold medal in the Skateboard Park competition, becoming the youngest champion in X Games history. She was only thirteen! She is currently one of sixteen members of the very first USA Skateboarding National Team. Brighton loves skateboarding for the freedom and creativity it gives her. And now she's using that creativity to help design new footwear for Vans.

THE ULTIMATE WOMEN IN SPORTS

Take this quiz to test your knowledge of *all* the amazing women throughout sports history.

1. Which swimmer won four golds at the 2012 Summer Olympics when she was just seventeen?

_____

2. Which gymnast, nicknamed the Flying Squirrel, was the first woman of color to win the all-around gold medal at the London 2012 Olympics?

_____

3. Who is the most successful female race car driver in Indy and NASCAR history?

_____

The Tokyo Games 2020

4. Who was born in Hawaii, attended Stanford University, and was the youngest golfer to qualify for an LPGA Tour event?

_____

5. Who did Emma Stone play in the 2017 film *Battle of the Sexes*?

_____

6. Which Romanian gymnast scored the first perfect 10 in Olympic competition?

_____

7. Can you name the iconic figure skater who won gold at the 1968 Olympics?

_____

8. Which 1996 Olympic gymnast famously vaulted while she was injured and had to be carried back to the bench by her coach, Bela Karolyi?

_____

9. Which American skier currently competing is the youngest slalom champion in Olympic alpine skiing history?

_____

10. Which swimmer won her final three career Olympic medals in 2008 at the age of forty-one, making her the oldest swimmer to win an Olympic medal?

_____

11. What sport did Martina Navratilova, Steffi Graf, and Margaret Court play?

_____

12. Which female boxing champ has a famous boxing dad who used to say, "Float like a butterfly, sting like a bee"?

_____

13. In what sport is Picabo Street an Olympic champion? _____

The Tokyo Games 2020

14. Which power forward for the Los Angeles Sparks was the first overall draft pick in the 2008 WNBA draft?

_____

15. Name the famous beach volleyball duo who won three consecutive Olympic gold medals starting in 2004.

_____

16. Which American figure skater beat Michelle Kwan for the 1988 Olympic gold when she was just fourteen years old?

_____

17. How old was Serena Williams when she turned pro?_____

18. Which 2000 Olympic track star was later stripped of her medals for steroid use?

_____

19. In what winter sport do Hannah Teter, Torah Bright, Chloe Kim, and Gretchen Bleiler compete?

_____

20. The 2017 film starring Margot Robbie about a figure skater whose husband orchestrates an attack on her skating rival is about which American skater?

_____

Check your answers on page 95. How'd you do?

1-5 correct: You're really an artist

6-10 correct: You're an amateur

11-15 correct: You're an Olympian

16-20 correct: You've gone pro

ANSWER KEY

TEST YOUR TENNIS CHOPS (PAGE 37)

1. California; 2. Billie Jean King; 3. Maureen "Little Mo" Connolly; 4. Australian Open, French Open, Wimbledon, US Open; 5. Ace; 6. Bianca Andreescu; 7. Althea Gibson; 8. Clay and grass; 9. Maria Sharapova; 10. 125 million

THE ULTIMATE WOMEN IN SPORTS (PAGE 90)

1. Missy Franklin; 2. Gabby Douglas; 3. Danica Patrick; 4. Michelle Wie; 5. Billie Jean King; 6. Nadia Comaneci; 7. Peggy Fleming; 8. Kerri Strug; 9. Mikaela Shiffrin; 10. Dara Torres; 11. Tennis; 12. Laila Ali; 13. Alpine skiing; 14. Candace Parker; 15. Kerri Walsh Jennings and Misty May-Treanor; 16. Tara Lipinski; 17. Fourteen; 18. Marion Jones; 19. Snowboarding; 20. Tonya Harding

HELP US PICK THE
NEXT ISSUE OF

HERE'S HOW TO VOTE:

Go to

www.ReadScoop.com

to cast your vote for who we should SCOOP! next.